M000048522

Instant Pot College Cookbook

Fast and Healthy Meals Made Right on Campus

**Tasty & Affordable Instant Pot Recipes
for Beginners College Students**

Tiffany Shelton

Copyright © 2020 by Tiffany Shelton.

All rights reserved.

No part of this book may be reproduced in any form or by any electronic or mechanical means, except in the case of a brief quotation embodied in articles or reviews, without written permission from its publisher.

Disclaimer

The recipes and information in this book are provided for educational purposes only. Please always consult a licensed professional before making changes to your lifestyle or diet. The author and publisher shall have neither liability nor responsibility to anyone with respect to any loss or damage caused or alleged to be caused directly or indirectly by the information contained in this book. All trademarks and brands within this book are for clarifying purposes only and are owned by the owners themselves, not affiliated with this document.

Images from shutterstock.com

CONTENTS

"The secrets of dorm chef:

how to live on a budget and be well fed at the same time"

INTRODUCTION

We all know how busy student life can be. Are you sick of KFC, McDonalds and other cheap junk food? Are you sick of a lack of energy? Are you dreaming of going back to your parents', not because you miss them but because of the delicious homemade meals?

For all our recipes you only need the Instant Pot! It helps people in creating culinary masterpieces in their kitchens, and our book gives you a chance to join them. Are you fond of French cuisine or Italian food? Maybe Chinese? Mexican? It's all here! Let us introduce you to satisfying your hunger with one pot!

With our book, it will be easier for you to get rid of hunger, forget about your bad mood, and ease digestive troubles.

CHAPTER 1. All about the instant pot

The Instant Pot is one of the most popular kitchen devices in our time. There are a lot of reasons why people prefer to use the pressure cooker:

✓ It saves time

The pressure cooker helps us to save time by doing the cooking for us. All you need to do is put the ingredients inside the pot and set it. While your little helper is busy, you're free to spend your time doing other important things or even rest. The Instant Pot will allows you to pressure-cook when you don't have time in the morning or slow-cook if you aren't in a hurry.

✓ It makes cooking easier

The Instant pot can replace several kitchen appliances at the same time, so you don't have to wash up a lot of dishes and pots anymore. Use a variety of modes and functions to cook only in one pot. It's perfect for pasta, vegetables, soups, any meat, and even desserts. Also, it cooks an endless amount of recipes faster than in the traditional way of cooking.

✓ It is healthy cooking

Scientific studies have confirmed that pressure cooking preserves more vitamins and increased antioxidant activity, making food easier to absorb by your body.

✓ It has a variety of cooking programs

The Instant Pot supports such programs as "soup," "meat/stew," "poultry," "bean/chili," "yogurt," and "rice."

✓ It is completely safe

You probably don't have a pressure cooker because of scary stories about how it can explode and cover the walls of your kitchen with mashed potatoes. We can't deny that it happened in the past, but now, in our time, it safe to use. The manufacturers have made great progress and improved their device to ensure user safety.

PLEASE REMEMBER THAT YOU'RE WORKING WITH PRESSURE!

Use the "Natural Release" method to let the Instant Pot release pressure for 15 minutes. Use the "Quick Release" method if you don't want to wait. Both methods are safe.

✓ It saves space

The Instant pot doesn't require much space, so it can be easily placed in kitchens of any size.

✓ It's reliable

You can trust your little helper with every meal, and it won't let you down. The pressure cooker won't spoil your meal thanks to its automatic mode and will keep your food warm while you're busy! You can trust it to cook during the night and won't be disappointed.

✓ It's user-friendly

At first sight, you may think that you will never get used to all the buttons on the display-panel. But it's much easier than you think! The more you use it, the easier it gets.

The simple construction of the device allows you to intuitively understand how it works and take care of it easily (to extend its life for many years).

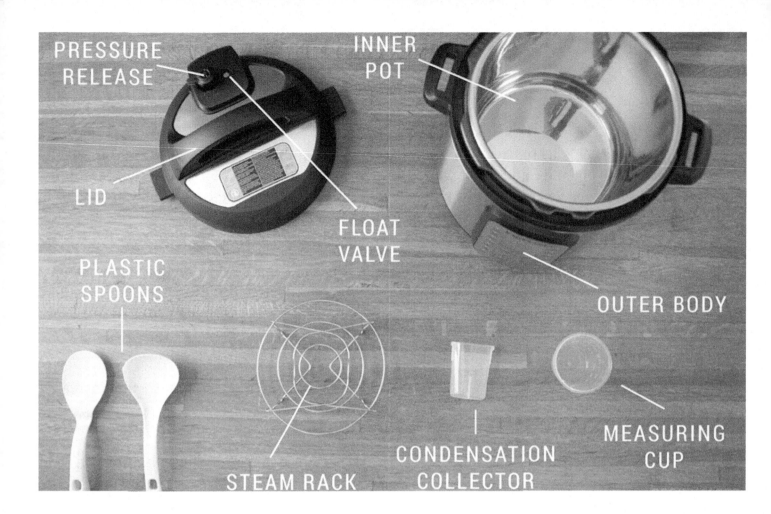

PRESSURE RELEASE · INNER POT · LID · FLOAT VALVE · PLASTIC SPOONS · OUTER BODY · STEAM RACK · CONDENSATION COLLECTOR · MEASURING CUP

Instant Pot Care & Cleaning

If you want to use the Instant Pot for a long time, you need to take care of it. The Instant Pot consists of many elements: steam release, inner pot, steam rack, and float valve, anti-block shield, sealing ring, lid, condensation cup.

If you cook in a pressure mode, you need to close **the steam release valve** or turn it to "pressure." If you cook in a slow mode, you need to open the valve to let steam escape.

The floating valve controls the pressure in the pot. It allows pressure to release during cooking.

The silicone gasket is the rubber ring set in a channel around the perimeter of the underside of the lid. You need to place the lid correctly to create an airtight seal.

The lid is needed to create an airtight seal when you locked the lid correctly on the pot.

The **locked lid indicator** shows you that the lid is locked. It is activated while pressure cooking. You can't open the lid when it is locked because of its danger.

The heating element controls the cooking temperature. It regulates the temperature of all modes.

The removable cooking pot can be made of aluminum or stainless steel, and often has a nonstick coating. Use only plastic accessories while cooking.

You set the cooking program with **the control panel.** From here, you control all of the processes and functions of the pressure cooker. Every model may have its own set of buttons, but all models will have an option for pressure and slow cooking, browning/sauteing. Use it to set a cook-timer and see the pot come up to pressure.

Now let's look at what should be washed regularly. Don't use a dishwasher!

Inner Pot

The inner pot is made of stainless steel, so you need to wash it in warm, soapy water. It should be washed after every cooking.

Steam Rack

Hand wash the steamer rack and dry it. It should be washed after every cooking too.

Steam Release Valve/float Valve

It gets dirtier after every preparation of food. Food particles may block the valves and make the Instant Pot work less effectively and may cause problems. So you must clean it.

Anti-block Shield

Remove the anti-block shield from the lid. Hand wash and dry it after wiping it with a soft towel. Before cooking, be sure it's placed correctly on the lid.

Sealing Ring

The rubber ring absorbs food odors, so you need to clean it regularly. Hand wash and dry it, then place it back on the lid. Be sure you did it correctly because it's very important to set it tight. Use separate rings for different meals: the first for savory foods and the second for sweet foods.

Outer body

Clean the outer body of your pressure cooker with a damp towel. There is the heating element inside the cooker, so you need to clean the inner body carefully. Use a damp towel and then dry it immediately.

Lid

Remove the anti-block shield and sealing ring, and then hand wash the lid. You don't have to clean it after every cooking, so wipe down the lid with a damp towel after meals.

Condensation Cup

Clean the cup from time to time when it becomes to get dirty.

Here some tips to refresh some parts of the pressure cooker and make them alive again!

Inner Pot

Pour one cup of white vinegar into the inner pot and leave for five minutes. Pour the vinegar out and wash the pot. If you want it to be shiny, use a non-abrasive scouring cleanser.

Sealing Ring

Add two teaspoons of lemon zest and two cups of water or white vinegar into the inner pot. Set to Steam mode for two minutes. Then remove the rubber ring and let it dry.

Instant Pot Settings

There are a lot of buttons on the display panel, so follow the instructions while you're cooking in the Instant Pot.

Manual/Pressure Cook:

If you need to cook on High Pressure, this is the button you need. Just press it, then use the [+]/ [-] buttons to change the cook time. Also, you can set the pressure level and cook time manually. Tap the [+]/[-] buttons to correct the setting.

Sauté:

This setting is perfect for browning meat (More), sauting the vegetables (Normal) and boiling (Low).

Soup/Broth:

Cook your meals for 30 minutes on High Pressure. Press More for 40 minutes. Press Less for 20 minutes.

Meat/Stew:

Cook your meals for 35 minutes on High Pressure. Press More for 45 minutes. Press Less for 20 minutes.

Bean/Chili:

Cook your meals for 30 minutes on High Pressure. Press More for 40 minutes. Press Less for 25 minutes.

Poultry:

Cook your meals for 15 minutes on High Pressure. Press More for 30 minutes. Press Less for 5 minutes.

Rice:

Adjust the cooking time depending on the amount of water and rice at Low Pressure. This is the only fully automatic program.

Multigrain:

Cook for 40 minutes on High Pressure. Press More for 60 minutes + 45 minutes of warm water soaking time. Press Less for 20 minutes.

Porridge:

Cooks your meals for 20 minutes on High Pressure. Press More for 30 minutes. Press Less for 15 minutes.

Steam:

Cooks your meals for 10 minutes on High Pressure. Press More for 15 minutes. Press Less for 3 minutes. Use only with a rack or steamer basket.

Less-Normal-More:

Tap the Less-Normal-More settings until you get the needed setting.

[-]/[+] Buttons:

Add [+] or reduce [-] cook time.

Slow Cook:

It has three temperature modes: low (180–190°F), normal (190–200°F), high (200–210°F). Press [-]/[+] to set the cook time.

Pressure Level:

You can choose High and Low Pressure cooking for your meals. It works with all modes that support High or Low Pressure cooking.

Keep Warm:

You can turn on Keep Warm mode to save the temperature of your meals.

Yogurt:

Press Normal for yogurt. Press More to boil the milk

Delay Start:

Set a cooking mode and time/pressure, tap Delay Start and use the [+]/[-] buttons to set time to wait for starting the cooking.

Cancel:

Cancel a selected cooking program. Also, you can reset the Instant Pot to default settings by holding this button.

Pressure Cook:

Chose High or Low Pressure and tap [+]/[-] buttons to set cook time. It starts to count down the time when the selected pressure level is reached.

Timer:

Set a cooking mode and time/pressure, press Timer and use the [+]/[-] buttons to set time to wait for starting the cooking.

CHAPTER 2. How to cook better with Instant Pot

Here we have some information for you about what you need to have in your kitchen. These things will improve the taste of your meals and also will improve your culinary skills

Sauces

Soy sauce: Of course, it is the most popular sauce in Asia. It's a must-have sauce for the lovers of its kitchen. There are three types of soy sauce: light soy sauce, dark soy sauce, thick soy sauce

Light soy sauce is thin and tastes salty, has a light brown color. The light soy sauce is often used for stir-fry meals, marinating, and dressings. Sometimes light soy sauce can be salty and have a deep taste. In this case, you can try to add a little bit of dark soy sauce to the light one and get an excellent combination.

Dark soy sauce is darker than light soy sauce, is thicker, and it tastes sweeter. It usually used in stew dishes. The sauce makes the meal sweeter for a little and gives it a nice caramel color.

Thick soy sauce is your choice for stir-fry meals and dips. Use it in stews and braised pork rice. You can use the oyster sauce if you don't have an opportunity to get the thick sauce.

Teriyaki sauce tastes like a mixture of soy sauce and honey and has a thick texture, even tangy. Use it to caramelize your meat and fish while roasting or browning it. Also, it makes the rice taste better.

Oyster sauce has a salty, sweet, and earthy taste. It is a well-known ingredient in Vietnam and Thailand.

Fish sauce has the fishy smell as cured anchovies. It is an important ingredient for authentic Asian taste of ramen, dipping sauces, and stir-fry. The fish sauce makes the taste of meals a little bit saltier and deeper.

Worcestershire sauce is a universal sauce with sweet and deep taste. It's used almost in all cuisines of the world for meat, fish, salads, soups, garnish and marinating.

Mustard has a lot of types of it: dijon, yellow, powdered, whole grain, and honey mustard. Use it to make the taste of your meat, vegetables or sauces piquant and sweeter

Ketchup. You can find it in every refrigerator. Most of the American recipes contain it, especially, meals like hamburgers, hot dogs, homemade barbecue, steaks, and others.

Vinegar is used in sauces, marinating and Asian rice recipes. It makes the taste more saturated and adds a little bit of piquancy. Also, you can use it for cleaning!

Hoisin sauce is a traditional sauce for Chinese meals (often served with the Peking duck). It is made of soybean paste with flavors and spices. The sauce has a sweet umami taste and tangy texture.

This chili oil is a must-have for lovers of chili or hot spicy food. It is perfect for dumplings, soups and noodles. Keep it in the dark and cool space in your kitchen.

Maple syrup with waffles is an incredible combination, just like tomatoes and basil. It also goes well with pancakes and other baked desserts. Add some tangy and sweet syrup in your breakfast to make it better!

Honey can be used for savory and sweet foods. Add it to your tea to make the taste sweet and domestic or glaze the meat to get a beautiful crust.

Spices

Black pepper: It is as essential as salt in your kitchen. You need a pepper grinder to use freshly ground powder because it's a way better than pre-ground one.

Paprika: It's made of chili peppers' dried fruits. Paprika is used to season meat, fish, seafood, vegetables, and soups. It gives the food lightly red or gold color.

Chili powder: One of the most important ingredients of Mexican and Southwestern cuisines. It's made of oregano, chilies, cumin, and coriander.

Curry powder: It is popular Indian mix of twenty or more spices such as turmeric, coriander, cumin, chili peppers, fenugreek. South Asian people use it for curry chicken, vegetables, soups, sauces, and salads.

Garlic Powder: The ground and dehydrated garlic powder is an alternative to fresh cloves. It is comfortable to use if you need to make a mix of spices for your dish. If you are tired of cleaning a garlic clover, use it!

Onion powder: You can use it for not to cry anymore while chopping the onion to your sauce. It can't be the full replacement of fresh onion but can be used for the spice mix.

Ground ginger: It is a hot, fragrant spice traditionally used in India, China, Japan, Vietnam, Thailand, and other South Asian countries. Ground ginger is often used to flavor cookies, crackers, cakes, and of course, gingerbread. It often goes with vegetables, meat, fish and also can be added to drinks cookies, cakes, and other desserts.

Bay leaves: Typically sold dried, bay leaves are aromatic with a woodsy taste. It's enough to add only one leaf to the meal because it's very potent. Use it with soups, sauces, marinates and dumplings.

Basil: The first of the main Italian spices. If you're an Italian food lover, you should have it on your shelf. It is often mixed with oregano, garlic, thyme, and tomato sauce. Basil is a traditional adding to rice, pasta, potato, and egg-based dishes. Keep the fresh and dried basil in your kitchen.

Oregano: The second of the main Italian spices. It has a bitter taste and a nice fragrance. It's better to use dried oregano than fresh. It goes with vegetables, meat, fish, and salads, barbecue recipes. Oregano is the main pizza flavor.

Rosemary: The third of the main Italian spices. It's usually used in Italy, France, and other Mediterranean countries. Rosemary goes well with olive oil and garlic. The taste is woody, has the fragrance of lemon and pine. It is traditional adding to Italian meals: focaccia, tomato sauce, pizza.

Thyme: It comes from Mediterranean and Cajun cuisines. The taste is a little bit woodsy that makes the vegetables, meat and poultry more interesting. It is always better to use fresh sprigs of thyme, but if you don't have them, use dried thyme.

Cinnamon: An aromatic stick or powder with a bittersweet taste, it can be used for drinks, savory and sweet foods. It is a very popular flavor in Asian cuisines: Indian, Chinese, Thai, and also in Mexican.

Vanilla extract: The most popular flavor for desserts: baked goods, ice cream, and syrups. It is made of the pods of the vanilla orchid. Vanilla extract is a must-have baking essential.

Accessories

<u>Stainless steel steamer basket</u> helps you to keep the vegetables, meat, fish out of the liquid for steaming in your pressure cooker. It makes the cooking more comfortable and easier.

<u>Silicone steamer basket</u> is perfect for if you don't like the stainless stell and want it to storage and clean it easily. Use it if the recipe require the food not to contact with the inner food.

<u>Stackable steamer pans</u> can be used for reheating leftovers in the pressure cooker.

<u>Glass lid</u> can be used while cooking on the non-pressurized modes on the pressure. Just the top of the inner pot. It will protect your kitchen from splattering while cooking on Saute mode. Also, it very useful for cooking on Slow (it won't your food dry).

<u>Silicone lid</u> allows you to keep your dishes in the inner pot. Cover it with the silicone lid and put to refrigerator.

<u>PLEASE REMEMBER!</u>

THE MAJORITY OF OUR RECIPES USE 6-QUART INSTANT POTS. IF YOU HAVE A DIFFERENT SIZE, PLEASE ADJUST THE RECIPES TO YOUR MODEL.

CHAPTER 3. Recipes

BREAKFAST

Vegetable Omelet

Prep time: 15 minutes

Cooking time: 30 minutes

Servings: 2

Nutrients per serving:

Carbohydrates – 6 g

Fat – 38 g

Protein – 25 g

Calories – 480 g

Ingredients:

- 6 eggs
- ¼ cup red bell pepper, chopped
- ¼ cup yellow onion, chopped
- ½ cup spinach
- 1 clove garlic
- 1 tsp oil
- ⅓ cup heavy cream
- ½ tsp salt
- ⅛ tsp pepper
- ½ cup grated cheddar cheese
- 1 cup water

Instructions:

1. Whisk together eggs and heavy cream.
2. Add salt and pepper and cheese.
3. Set to Sauté and heat the oil.
4. Sauté onion and pepper. When tender, add garlic and spinach.
5. Add cooked vegetables to the prepared mixture. Switch IP off.
6. Add water. Add with a handled trivet.
7. Pour mixture into the pan. Place on top of trivet and lock the lid.
8. Set to 6 minutes of high pressure.
9. Release for 10-12 minutes.
10. Enjoy!

Light Burritos

Prep time: 3 minutes

Cooking time: 35 minutes

Servings: 10

Nutrients per serving:

Carbohydrates – 18 g

Fat – 16 g

Protein – 12 g

Calories – 264

Ingredients:

- 2½ cups hash brown potatoes
- 1 cup diced ham
- 6 eggs
- ¼ cup milk
- ¼ cup sour cream
- ½ cup shredded cheese
- 10 tortillas
- ¼ tsp salt
- ⅛ tsp pepper

Instructions:

1. Spray pot with cooking spray to avoid sticking.
2. Place hash browns into the small liner.
3. Put ham on top of the hash browns.
4. Mix eggs, milk, sour cream, cheese, salt and pepper in a separate bowl.
5. Pour mixture over the hash browns and ham.

6. Cover with foil.
7. Pour a cup of water in a larger liner and put inside the trivet.
8. Put the smaller pot on the trivet.
9. Set to 25 minutes of high pressure (manual).
10. Quick-release, take the foil off to stir, replace the foil.
11. Set to 10 minutes of high pressure (manual).
12. Release the pressure.
13. Stuff the filling into tortillas.
14. Enjoy!

Perfect eggs

Prep time: 10 minutes

Cooking time: 5 minutes

Servings: 1

Nutrients per serving:

Carbohydrates –1 g

Fat – 11 g

Protein – 13 g

Calories – 160

Ingredients

- 2 eggs
- 1 cup water

Instructions:

1. Pour the water into the pot.
2. Put the eggs into a steamer basket.
3. Close the lid.
4. Set to 5 minutes of high pressure.
5. Let the pressure release (5 minutes).
6. Quick-release the rest pressure.
7. Put the hot eggs into water with ice to make peeling easier.
8. Enjoy!

Oatmeal with Apples and Honey

Prep time: 5 minutes

Cooking time: 20 minutes

Servings: 4

Nutrients per serving:

Carbohydrates – 16 g

Fat – 5 g

Protein – 3 g

Calories – 134

Ingredients:

- 1 cup steel-cut oats
- 3 cups of water
- ½ cup chopped apples
- 1 tsp ground cinnamon
- 1-2 tsp honey
- ½ tsp butter

Instructions:

1. Spray the inner pot to avoid sticking.
2. Add oats to the pot.
3. Add water to the pot.
4. Stir in apples and cinnamon.
5. Lock the lid and set to Sealing.
6. Set to 4 minutes (manual).
7. When oats are cooked, let it release (10-15 minutes).
8. Unlock the lid and stir oatmeal.
9. Add honey.
10. Enjoy!

Ginger Oatmeal

Prep time: 10 minutes

Cooking time: 20 minutes

Servings: 6

Nutrients per serving:

Carbohydrates – 39 g

Fat – 4 g

Protein – 7 g

Calories – 208

Ingredients:

- 1¼ cups steel-cut oats
- 15 ounces solid-pack pumpkin
- 1½ tsp pumpkin pie spice
- 3 tbsp brown sugar
- 1 tsp ground cinnamon
- ¾ tsp salt
- 3 cups of water

Instructions:

1. Put oats, spice, pumpkin, sugar, cinnamon, salt and water in a pressure pot.
2. Lock lid and close the vent.
3. Set to 10 minutes of high pressure (manual).
4. When cooked, let the pressure to release for 10 minutes.
5. Quick-release the rest pressure.
6. Stir in pumpkin.
7. Let stand 5-10 minutes to thicken.
8. Enjoy!

Cinnamon Roll Oatmeal

Prep time: 5 minutes

Cooking time: 10

Servings: 1

Nutrients per serving:

Carbohydrates – 66 g

Fat – 11 g

Protein – 7 g

Calories – 373

Ingredients:

- 1 cup steel-cut oats
- 3½ cups water
- ¼ tsp salt
- ¾ cup raisins
- ¼ cup brown sugar
- 1 tsp cinnamon
- 2 ounces cream cheese
- 2 tbsp powdered sugar
- 1 tsp milk
- 1 cup water

Instructions:

1. Add butter to pressure pot.
2. Program to Sauté.
3. Add the oats and toast, stirring, until they start to darken and smell nutty, about 3 minutes.
4. Add water and salt.
5. Set 10 minutes of high pressure.
6. Turn off when the cooking is done.
7. Let it release (5 minutes) and then do a quick pressure release.
8. Add raisins and stir the oats.
9. Cover and let stand for 5-10 minutes to thicken.
10. Enjoy!

Big Boy Pancake

Prep time: 5 minutes

Cooking time: 45 minutes

Servings: 1

Nutrients per serving:

Carbohydrates – 59 g

Fat – 3 g

Protein – 12 g

Calories – 320

Ingredients:

- 2 cups flour
- 2½ tsp baking powder
- 2 tbsp white sugar
- 2 eggs
- 1½ cups milk

Instructions:

1. Whisk eggs and milk until completely blended.
2. Add remaining ingredients and whisk until only very small lumps remain in the butter.
3. Grease the interior of the instant pot with oil.
4. Close the lid and the vent.
5. Set to 45 minutes of low pressure (manual) to get a brown top.
6. Check on the cake when it's done (it should bounce back with cooked batter and the cake should pull away from the sides).
7. If the cake isn't quite done, let go on cooking it on low pressure for a few more minutes.
8. Serve.

Sweet Maple Bites

Prep time: 10 minutes

Cooking time: 35 minutes

Servings: 6

Nutrients per serving:

Carbohydrates – 19 g

Fat – 17 g

Protein – 14 g

Calories – 378

Ingredients:

- 1½ cup cubed bread
- ½ cup cream cheese
- 4 eggs
- ½ cup milk
- ¼ cup maple syrup

Instructions:

1. Put bread in a greased 1½ qt. baking dish.
2. Top with cream cheese.
3. Whisk together eggs, milk, and syrup.
4. Pour over bread and let stand 30 minutes.
5. Put trivet inside and 1 cup water in a pressure cooker.
6. Cover the dish with foil (use the sling to lower dish into pressure cooker).
7. Set to 20 minutes of high pressure.
8. Release pressure for 10 minutes.
9. Quick-release the rest pressure.
10. Enjoy!

Blueberry Mini Cakes

Prep time: 5 minutes

Cooking time: 8 minutes

Servings: 3

Nutrients per serving:

Carbohydrates – 23 g

Fat – 3 g

Protein – 3 g

Calories – 138

Ingredients:

- 1 cup pancake mix
- 1 cup water
- ½ cup blueberries
- 2 tbsp brown sugar

Instructions:

1. Pour water into Instant Pot, and lower trivet inside the pot.
2. Whisk together pancake mix, sugar and water.
3. Add blueberries.
4. Fill egg mold with butter (¾ full).
5. Cover with foil, and put down into pot on top of the trivet.
6. Set to 8 minutes of high pressure.
7. Let it release (5 minutes).
8. Let cool before serving.
9. Enjoy!

Sweet Banana Cake

Prep time: 15 minutes

Cooking time: 50 minutes

Servings: 12

Nutrients per serving:

Carbohydrates – 34 g

Fat – 8 g

Protein – 3 g

Calories – 227

Ingredients:

- 2¼ cups mashed bananas
- 2 cups flour
- ¼ tsp salt
- 1 tsp baking soda
- ½ tsp nutmeg
- ½ cup butter
- ¼ cup white sugar
- ¼ cup brown sugar
- 2 eggs
- 1 tsp vanilla
- 1 tsp cinnamon

Instructions:

1. Mash bananas.
2. Mix the flour, salt, baking soda, and nutmeg in a bowl#1.
3. Mix butter, brown and white sugar in bowl#2.
4. Add to bowl#2 eggs, cinnamon, mashed bananas, then add this mixture to flour (bowl#1) and stir.
5. Pour butter into a greased pan.
6. Insert a trivet and add water into the pot.
7. Cover your pan with foil.
8. Set to 50 minutes (manual). When finished, do a quick-release on the pot.
9. Remove the pan from the pot and let it cool.
10. Enjoy!

SOUPS

Light Chicken Soup

Prep time: 25 minutes

Cooking time: 20 minutes

Servings: 6

Nutrients per serving:

Carbohydrates – 21 g

Fat – 3 g

Protein – 3 g

Calories – 129

Ingredients:

- 1 tbsp olive oil
- 5 medium carrots
- 3 stalks celery
- 2 cloves garlic
- 1 large yellow onion
- 1 3-lb whole chicken
- 8 cups of water
- 1 tbsp salt
- 1 large pinch ground black pepper
- 3 cups egg noodles

Instructions:

1. Set to Saute (high).
2. Heat the oil, and add the carrots, celery, garlic, onion, salt, black pepper. Cook for 5 minutes.
3. Add chicken and water.
4. Set to 20 minutes of high pressure (manual).
5. Quick-release the pressure when it finished.
6. Remove the cover when the valve drops.
7. Remove chicken and let cool.
8. Remove the skin and bones and shred the meat.
9. Set to high Sauté and let the soup boil.
10. Add noodles and cook 4-5 minutes.
11. Add the chicken and stir the soup.
12. Enjoy!

Chilli Bowl

Prep time: 25 minutes

Cooking time: 20 minutes

Servings: 6

Nutrients per serving:

Carbohydrates – 24 g

Fat – 16 g

Protein – 24 g

Calories – 343

Ingredients:

- ¾ pound boneless skinless chicken breasts
- ¼ tsp salt
- ¼ tsp pepper
- 2 tbsp oil
- 1 onion
- 1 jalapeno pepper
- 4 garlic cloves
- 2 tsp dried oregano
- 1 tsp ground cumin
- 30 ounces cannellini beans
- 2½ cups chicken broth
- 1½ cups shredded cheese
- chopped parsley

Instructions:

1. Set to Saute (medium heat).
2. Heat the oil.
3. Cook chicken till brown and set aside.
4. Add salt and pepper.
5. Saute onion, jalapeno, garlic, oregano, cumin. Cook 2 minutes and press Cancel.
6. Return chicken to pot.
7. In a bowl, mash 1 cup beans; stir in ½ cup broth.
8. Add mashed beans, whole beans, and broth to chicken.
9. Lock the lid and the valve.
10. Set to 10 minutes of high pressure.
11. When finished, quick-release pressure.
12. Stir the soup well.
13. Serve with cheese and parsley.
14. Enjoy!

Mexican Chicken Soup

Prep time: 20 minutes

Cooking time: 15 minutes

Servings: 6

Nutrients per serving:

Carbohydrates – 9 g

Fat – 15 g

Protein – 19 g

Calories – 257

Ingredients:

- 1 pound boneless, skinless chicken breasts
- 2 tbs oil
- 2 jalapenos
- 1 small onion
- 2 cloves garlic
- ½ tsp cumin
- 1 tbs chili powder
- 1½ cups salsa
- 1 tsp salt
- ½ tsp pepper
- 3 cups chicken stock
- ½ block cream cheese

Instructions:

1. Set to Saute and heat the oil.
2. Add vegetables and spices. Saute for 2-3 minutes, stirring often.
3. Turn off Saute.
4. Add chicken, salsa, and chicken stock.
5. Lock the lid and turn to Sealing.
6. Cook for 5 minutes.
7. Let the pressure to release when it's done.
8. Shred the chicken.
9. Add cream cheese and let it melt.
10. Stir the soup well.
11. Enjoy!

Chicken Broth

Prep time: 10 minutes

Cooking time: 45 minutes

Servings: 6 cups

Nutrients per serving:

Carbohydrates – 2 g

Fat – 0 g

Protein – 4 g

Calories – 25

Ingredients:

- 2½ pounds bony chicken pieces
- 2 celery ribs with leaves
- 2 medium carrots
- 2 medium onions
- 2 bay leaves
- ½ tsp dried rosemary, crushed
- ½ tsp dried thyme
- 8-10 whole peppercorns
- 6 cups cold water

Instructions:

1. Put all ingredients into the instant pot.
2. Lock the lid and close the vent.
3. Set to 45 minutes of high pressure (manual).
4. Release the pressure when it finished.
5. Remove chicken and set aside for use in other meals.
6. Strain the broth with a sieve.
7. Refrigerate overnight.
8. Remove the layer of fat from the surface.
9. Enjoy!

CHICKEN

Mexican Style Chicken

Prep time: 5 minutes

Cooking time: 35 minutes

Servings: 2

Nutrients per serving:

Carbohydrates – 14 g

Fat – 5 g

Protein – 50 g

Calories – 300

Ingredients:

- 1 pound skinless, boneless chicken breast
- 2 Tbsp taco seasoning mix
- ½ cup salsa
- ½ cup chicken broth
- a pinch of chopped parsley

Instructions:

1. Seasone the chicken breasts with taco seasoning mix an put it into the bottom of the pot.
2. Pour salsa and chicken broth over the chicken.
3. Lock the lid.
4. Set to 15 minutes (Poultry).
5. Let the pressure release for 20-25 minutes when it's done.
6. Shred the cooked chicken.
7. Serve with chopped parsley.
8. Enjoy!

Easy Chicken Breasts

Prep time: 10 minutes

Cooking time: 3 hours

Servings: 6

Nutrients per serving:

Carbohydrates – 4 g

Fat – 33 g

Protein – 7 g

Calories – 339

Ingredients:

- 1 cup chicken broth
- 1 pound skinless, boneless chicken breast
- ½ tsp paprika
- ½ tsp parsley
- ¼ tsp dried thyme
- ¼ tsp garlic powder
- Salt to taste
- Black pepper to taste

Instructions:

1. Pour chicken broth into the bottom of the pressure cooker.
2. Combine spices and season breasts.
3. Put them into the broth.
4. Lock the lid.
5. Set to 10 minutes of high pressure.
6. Let the pressure release when it finishes cooking.
7. Enjoy!

Chicken with Baby Potatoes

Prep time: 10 minutes

Cooking time: 30 minutes

Servings: 4

Nutrients per serving:

Carbohydrates – 28 g

Fat – 13 g

Protein – 27 g

Calories – 359

Ingredients:

- 1 pound boneless skinless chicken breasts
- 2 pounds baby red or gold potatoes
- 3 tbsp olive oil
- 1½ tsp salt
- ½ tsp pepper
- 1 tsp garlic powder
- 1 tsp dried thyme
- ½ tsp dried basil
- ½ tsp dried oregano
- 1 cup chicken broth

Instructions:

1. Grease chicken and potatoes with oil.
2. Mix all spices and season the chicken and potatoes with it.
3. Pour the broth into the instant pot.
4. Put the chicken in the broth and cover with the potatoes.
5. Lock the lid and close the vent.
6. Set to 15 minutes (pressure cook).
7. Quick-release when finished cooking.
8. Enjoy!

Chicken with Garlic Sauce

Prep time: 5 minutes

Cooking time: 15 minutes

Servings: 4

Nutrients per serving:

Carbohydrates – 16 g

Fat – 32 g

Protein – 29 g

Calories – 268

Ingredients:

- 1 tbsp oil
- 4 chicken thighs
- 4 cloves garlic
- 3 tbsp honey
- 1 tsp sugar
- 2 tbsp soy sauce
- 3 tbsp water or chicken broth
- 3 dashes cayenne pepper
- Black pepper to taste
- Salt to taste
- a pinch of chopped parsley

Instructions:

1. Combine soy sauce, honey, sugar together.
2. Season the meat with salt, cayenne and black pepper, set aside.
3. Set to Saute mode and heat the oil.
4. Brown both sides of chicken thighs, skin side down first.
5. Add and saute the garlic for a few minutes.
6. Pour in the sauce mixture.
7. Lock the lid and close the vent.
8. Set to 10 minutes of high pressure (manual).
9. Quick-release the pressure when it's done.
10. Sprinkle with parsley and enjoy!

Creamy Piquant Chicken

Prep time: 15 minutes

Cooking time: 15 minutes

Servings: 6

Nutrients per serving:

Carbohydrates – 17 g

Fat – 26 g

Protein – 28 g

Calories – 430

Ingredients:

- 3 pounds boneless, skinless chicken breast
- ½ onion
- 4 garlic cloves
- ⅓ cup chicken broth
- 2 tbsp heavy cream
- 4 tbsp olive oil
- ¾ tsp garlic powder
- ¾ tsp paprika
- ¾ tsp red pepper flakes
- 2 tsp salt
- 1 tsp ground pepper
- 2 tbsp Italian seasoning
- Juice and zest of 1 lemon

Instructions:

1. Combine all spices and use to season the chicken.
2. Set to Saute and heat the oil.
3. Brown chicken breasts and set them aside.
4. Add and saute onion and garlic for a few minutes.
5. Add spice mixture, lemon juice, zest and stir.
6. Pour in chicken broth and stir again.
7. Put the chicken back in the pot.
8. Lock the lid and set the valve to Sealing.
9. Set to 7 minutes (manual).
10. When it's finished, quick-release.
11. Take the chicken out.
12. Set to Saute and add the heavy cream.
13. Let the sauce thicken, 2-4 minutes.
14. Put the chicken back and cover it with the lemon garlic sauce.
15. Enjoy!

Chicken and Vegetable Rice

Prep time: 20 minutes

Cooking time: 20 minutes

Servings: 6

Nutrients per serving:

Carbohydrates – 47 g

Fat – 8 g

Protein – 30 g

Calories – 378

Ingredients:

- 1 tbsp olive oil
- 1 cup chopped onion
- 4 medium carrots
- 3 cloves garlic minced
- 1½ cups brown rice
- 2 tsp dried Italian seasoning
- 1½ tsp garlic powder
- ½ tsp salt
- ¼ tsp black pepper
- 1½ cups chicken broth
- 1 pound boneless skinless chicken breasts
- 1 cup frozen peas

Instructions:

1. Set to Saute mode and heat the oil.
2. Add and saute onion and carrots for 5 minutes.
3. Add spices, garlic, and rice. Cook for 3-4 minutes, stirring.
4. Press Cancel.
5. Pour in the chicken broth and stir.
6. Put the breasts on top of the rice.
7. Lock the lid and set the valve to Sealing.
8. Set for 20 minutes of high pressure.
9. Let it release for 15 minutes when done cooking.
10. Quick-release the remaining steam and pressure.
11. Take out the meat and shred it.
12. Put it back into the rice with the peas.
13. Let it release for 12 minutes.
14. Enjoy!

Chicken and Broccoli

Prep time: 10 minutes

Cooking time: 10 minutes

Servings: 4

Nutrients per serving:

Carbohydrates – 8 g

Fat – 23 g

Protein – 22 g

Calories – 387

Ingredients:

- 2 tsp oil
- 1 pound of boneless chicken tenderloins
- ½ cup shallots
- 2 cloves of garlic
- 1 tsp grated ginger
- ⅔ cup chicken stock
- ⅓ cup of soy sauce
- 2 tbsp plus 1 tsp honey
- 3½ cups of broccoli florets
- ½ tbsp flour
- 2 scallions, chopped
- ¼ tsp salt
- 1 tsp crushed red pepper

Instructions:

1. Blend soy sauce, chicken stock, honey and ginger together.
2. Set to Saute and heat the oil.
3. Saute shallots until they begin to soften and become fragrant.
4. Add garlic and stir.

5. Pour in the stock and add chicken.
6. Lock the lid and set to 7 minutes (manual).
7. When it's done, do a quick release.
8. Take out the meat and set it aside.
9. Remove 1 cup of the cooking liquid and add the flour to it.
10. Mix it well and add it back to the pot.
11. Set to Sauté to make the sauce thicker.
12. Stir in salt and turn to Keep Warm.
13. Add chicken and chopped broccoli florets and stir.
14. Cover the pot for 10 minutes.
15. Serve and enjoy!

Tomato Chicken

Prep time: 10 minutes

Cooking time: 5 minutes

Servings: 6

Nutrients per serving:

Carbohydrates – 9 g

Fat – 50 g

Protein – 20 g

Calories – 574

Ingredients:

- 6 boneless, skinless chicken thighs
- 1½ cup heavy cream
- 1½ cup tomato sauce
- ½ onion
- 5 tbsp butter
- 1 tbsp garlic minced
- 1 tbsp ginger chopped
- 1½ tsp chili powder
- 1½ tsp cumin
- 1 tsp garam masala

Instructions:

1. Set to Saute and heat the butter.
2. Add and saute chicken and onion till the meat is well-done.
3. Stir in remaining ingredients.
4. Lock the lid and close the valve.
5. Set to 5 minutes of low pressure.
6. When finished, let the pot release for a few minutes.
7. Quick-release the rest pressure.
8. Serve and enjoy!

Browned Chicken Thighs

Prep time: 10 minutes

Cooking time: 35 minutes

Servings: 4

Nutrients per serving:

Carbohydrates – 7 g

Fat – 21 g

Protein – 37 g

Calories – 370

Ingredients:

- 2 pounds chicken thighs
- ½ cup soy sauce
- ⅓ cup white vinegar
- 1 onion
- 5 cloves garlic
- 1 tbsp oil
- ¼ tsp cayenne
- salt and coarse black pepper to taste

Instructions:

1. Set to Saute (medium).
2. Season chicken thighs with salt and pepper.
3. Heat the oil and brown chicken thighs on both sides. Set them aside.
4. Press Cancel.
5. Blend together soy sauce, vinegar, onion, garlic, and cayenne.
6. Clean the pot of any brown bits.
7. Put the thighs in one layer inside the pot.
8. Pour the sauce mixture over the chicken.
9. Lock the lid.
10. Set to 10 minutes of high pressure (manual).
11. Unlock the lid and set to Saute.
12. Boil chicken in the pot for 15 minutes to thicken the sauce.
13. Enjoy!

Chicken

Prep time: 10 minutes

Cooking time: 40 minutes

Servings: 4

Nutrients per serving:

Carbohydrates – 4 g

Fat – 46 g

Protein – 32 g

Calories – 500

Ingredients:

- 1 whole chicken
- 1 onion
- 1 tbsp olive oil
- ½ cups of water
- 1 tsp dried herbs
- 1 tsp salt
- ½ tsp black pepper
- ½ tsp garlic powder

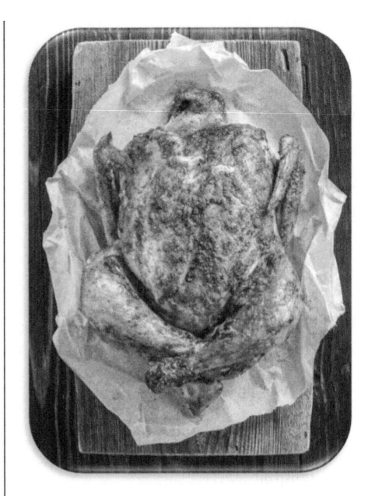

Instructions:

1. Pour 1½ cups of water into the pressure cooker pot.
2. Put a trivet inside.
3. Dry the chicken with paper towels.
4. Smear the chicken with oil and all spices.
5. Put the bird on top of the trivet in the pot, breast side up.
6. Evenly distribute chopped onions on top of the chicken.
7. Lock the lid and close the vent.
8. Set to 25 minutes of high pressure.
9. When finished, let it release the pressure (15-20 minutes).
10. Take the chicken out of the pot.
11. Take some liquid from the pot and cover chicken with it. Enjoy!

BEEF AND PORK

Beef Stew

Prep time: 20 minutes

Cooking time: 20

Servings: 10

Nutrients per serving:

Carbohydrates – 20 g

Fat – 14 g

Protein – 4 g

Calories – 395

Ingredients:

- 1½-2 pounds beef chuck roast
- 1-2 tsp salt
- ½ tsp black pepper
- ½ tsp dried oregano
- 1 tsp dried thyme
- ½ tsp dried rosemary
- ⅓ cup flour
- 2 tbsp oil
- 1 onion
- 3-4 cloves garlic
- 6 tbsp tomato paste
- 1 pound Guinness Extra Stout
- 4 Yukon potatoes
- 1 carrot
- 1 celery rubs
- 1-2 tsp Worcestershire sauce
- 1 bay leaf
- 2 cups beef broth
- Water, as needed to cover the vegetables
- ½ cup peas

Instructions:

1. Mix all spices with the flour.
2. Dredge the meat in the flour.
3. Set to Saute and heat the oil.
4. Brown all sides of the beef and set it aside.
5. Add and saute the onion and garlic for a few minutes.
6. Add Guinness and tomato paste.
7. Put the meat back into the pot.
8. Add remaining ingredients (except peas) and stir well.
9. Cover the vegetables with water.
10. Lock the lid and set to 20 minutes high pressure (manual).
11. Let it release (15 minutes).
12. Add the peas and mix well.
13. Enjoy!

Beef with Creamy Mushroom Sauce

Prep time: 20 minutes

Cooking time: 15 minutes

Servings: 4

Nutrients per serving:

Carbohydrates – 18 g

Fat – 10 g

Protein – 10 g

Calories – 208

Ingredients:

- 3 tsp oil
- 2 pound beef top sirloin steak
- ½ tsp salt
- ¼ tsp pepper
- ⅓ beef broth
- ½ pound baby portobello mushrooms
- 1 small onion, halved and sliced
- 1 cup beef broth
- 1 tbsp Worcestershire sauce
- 1-4 tbsp cornstarch (depends of thickness)
- ¼ cup of water

Instructions:

1. Set to Saute (medium heat) and heat the oil.
2. Season the meat with salt and pepper.
3. Brown it and set aside.
4. Pour the broth into the pot and turn the cooker off.
5. Put back the meat and add mushrooms, onion, broth, and Worcestershire sauce.
6. Lock lid and valve.
7. Set to 15 minutes of high pressure.
8. When it's done, do a quick-release.
9. Set to Saute (low heat) and let it boil.
10. Combine cornstarch and water until smooth and add it slowly into the pot.
11. Cook and stir until sauce is thickened.
12. Enjoy!

Beer Club Beef

Prep time: 15 minutes

Cooking time: 20 minutes

Servings: 4

Nutrients per serving:

Carbohydrates – 9 g

Fat – 25 g

Protein – 12 g

Calories – 284

Ingredients:

- 4 pound fresh beef brisket
- 2 tsp liquid smoke
- 1 tsp celery salt
- ½ tsp pepper
- ¼ tsp salt
- 1 large onion
- 0,75 pound beer
- 2 tsp Worcestershire sauce
- 2 tbsp cornstarch
- ¼ cup of water

Instructions:

1. Prepare brisket: season it with salt and pepper and cut in half.
2. Put the brisket into the pot fat side down.
3. Mix the beer and Worcestershire sauce.
4. Pour the mixture over the meat.
5. Lock the lid and the valve.
6. Set to 1 hour 10 minutes high pressure.
7. Let it release for 10 minutes.

8. Do a quick-release.
9. If you can't shred the meat with forks, cook it for 10-15 minutes more.
10. Take out the meat.
11. Strain the juices from the meat and back it to the pot.
12. Set to Saute (medium heat).
13. Let the liquid come to a boil.
14. Combine cornstarch and water and add it slowly into the pot.
15. Let the sauce thicken.
16. Enjoy!

Beef with Stewed Vegetables

Prep time: 20 minutes

Cooking time: 35 minutes

Servings: 4

Nutrients per serving:

Carbohydrates – 20 g

Fat – 21 g

Protein – 30 g

Calories – 416

Ingredients:

- 1 pound beef chuck roast
- ⅔ cup chicken broth
- 1 onion
- 8 ounces baby potatoes
- 3 carrots
- 1 tbsp olive oil
- 1 tbsp tomato paste
- 1 tbsp Worcestershire sauce
- 1 tsp onion powder
- 1 tsp garlic powder
- 1 tsp ground black pepper
- 1 tsp salt
- ½ tsp dried thyme

Instructions:

1. Set to 15 minutes Saute and heat the oil.
2. Mix all spices and use mixture to season meat.
3. Brown the beef on all sides and set it aside.
4. Add the tomato paste, Worcestershire sauce, and broth.
5. Stir the mixture well and put the beef back.
6. Press Cancel.
7. Set to 35 minutes of high pressure.
8. Arrange the vegetables around the meat.
9. Lock the lid and set the valve to Sealing.
10. When it's done, let it release.
11. Enjoy!

Beef Spaghetti Balls

Prep time: 10 minutes

Cooking time: 10 minutes

Servings: 6

Nutrients per serving:

Carbohydrates – 15 g

Fat – 27 g

Protein –28 g

Calories – 411

Ingredients:

- 1½ pounds lean ground beef
- ½ cup onion grated
- ½ cup panko bread crumbs
- 2 eggs
- 2 cloves garlic crushed
- 2 tbsps milk
- 1 tsp salt
- ½ tsp oregano
- ¼ tsp ground black pepper
- 4 cup spaghetti sauce

Instructions:

1. Combine all ingredients except the sauce in a large bowl and mix well by hand.
2. Form into balls.
3. Spray the inner pot with cooking spray.
4. Pour in the spaghetti sauce.
5. Put the meatballs into the sauce.
6. Lock the lid and seal the valve.
7. Set to 7 minutes of high pressure (manual).
8. Let it naturally release the pressure when it's done.
9. Do quick-release.
10. Enjoy!

Roast Baby Back Ribs

Prep time: 25 minutes

Cooking time: 30 minutes

Servings: 6

Nutrients per serving:

Carbohydrates – 24 g

Fat – 32 g

Protein – 18 g

Calories – 462

Ingredients:

- 1 rack baby back ribs
- ¼ cup brown sugar
- 2 tsp salt
- 2 tsp paprika
- 1 cup apple juice

Instructions:

1. Combine all spices and use mixture to season the ribs.
2. Put the trivet into the pot.
3. Pour in the cup of apple juice.
4. Put the ribs on the trivet.
5. Lock the lid and set to 25 minutes of high pressure.
6. Let it release the pressure (15-20 minutes).
7. Enjoy!

Juicy Pork Chops

Prep time: 20 minutes

Cooking time: 20 minutes

Servings: 4

Nutrients per serving:

Carbohydrates – 13 g

Fat – 22 g

Protein – 53 g

Calories – 470

Ingredients:

- 4 bone-in well-marbled pork loin center chops
- 2 tbsp butter
- 8-12 cremini mushrooms
- ¾ cup unsalted chicken stock
- 2 tbsp soy sauce
- 1 onion
- 4 garlic cloves
- ½ tsp dried thyme
- ½ tsp dried rosemary
- salt and pepper to taste
- 2 tbsp flour
- ½ cup heavy cream

Instructions:

1. Score criss-cross patterns into both sides of the meat.
2. Sprinkle one side of the meat with salt and pepper.
3. Put into the pot and set to Saute for 8-10 minutes.
4. Add the butter to the pot.
5. Brown seasoned sides of 2 chops and set aside. Repeat it for other 2 chops.
6. Saute onion, mushrooms and garlic.
7. Add dried thyme and rosemary and cook for a few minutes.
8. Pour in chicken stock and soy sauce.
9. Put browned pork chops into the pot.
10. Lock the lid and turn vent to Sealing.
11. Set to 0 (zero) minutes high pressure
12. Let it release for 10 minutes.
13. Combine all-purpose flour with heavy cream.
14. Take out the meat and let the liquid boil in Sauce mode.
15. Add heavy cream to make the sauce thicker and cook for 2-3 minutes.
16. Enjoy!

Soft Pork Loin

Prep time: 10 minutes

Cooking time: 1 hour 15 minutes

Servings: 6

Nutrients per serving:

Carbohydrates – 10 g

Fat – 21 g

Protein – 40 g

Calories – 363

Ingredients:

- 4 tbsp butter
- 1½ pound pork loin
- 1 onion, chopped
- 2¼ cup chicken broth

Instructions:

1. Set to Saute and heat the butter
2. Cook the seasoned pork loin for 4 minutes.
3. Flip the meat, add onion and let cook for 5 minutes.
4. Cover the meat with chicken broth.
5. Set to 35 minutes of high pressure.
6. Let it release.
7. Take out the meat and let it rest.
8. Enjoy!

Irish Pork Shoulder

Prep time: 20 minutes

Cooking time: 40 minutes

Servings: 4-6

Nutrients per serving:

Carbohydrates – 15 g

Fat – 27 g

Protein – 32 g

Calories – 403

Ingredients:

- 1 pound pork shoulder
- 2 tbsp oil
- 2 cups chicken broth or water
- 1 onion, chopped
- 3 cloves garlic
- 1½ tsp salt
- 1½ tsp pepper
- 1 tsp garlic powder

Instructions:

1. Mix all the spices.
2. Rub oil over pork and season with spice mixture.
3. Set to Sauté and heat the oil.
4. Brown each side of the meat, 4-5 minutes per side.
5. Set pork aside and press Cancel.
6. Pour in the broth and put the trivet inside the pressure cooker.
7. Put the meat on the trivet and add onion and garlic.
8. Lock the lid and set the valve to Sealing.
9. Set to 30 minutes Stew.
10. Let it release for 10 minutes,
11. Quick-release the remaining pressure.
12. Enjoy!

FISH

Healthy Fish

Prep time: 10 minutes

Cooking time: 4 minutes

Servings: 4

Nutrients per serving:

Carbohydrates – 41 g

Fat – 17 g

Protein – 24 g

Calories – 418

Ingredients:

- 1 cup basmati rice
- 1 pound frozen haddock fillets
- 2 cups frozen spinach
- 1 cup of water
- 3 tbsp oil
- 1 tsp salt
- 1-tsp ground pepper
- Sesame seeds

Instructions:

1. Cut the fillets into 4 pieces
2. Rinse the rice in cold water 7 times.
3. Place the rice, water, salt, and oil into the pot and stir it.
4. Cut 4 pieces of foil to wrap the fish in a pocket.
5. Put spinach on each of the four sheets.
6. Put the fish on top.
7. Season the fish with oil, salt and pepper.
8. Close up the pockets to not to leak.
9. Place a steamer rack on top of the rice.
10. Place the aluminum packets of spinach and fish on the steamer rack in one layer.
11. Set to 4 minutes high pressure.
12. Let it release the pressure (10 minutes)
13. Do a quick release next.
14. Serve the fish on top of the rice with spinach.
15. Sprinkle with sesame seeds.
16. Enjoy!

Asian Style White Fish

Prep time: 10 minutes

Cooking time: 10 minutes

Servings: 4

Nutrients per serving:

Carbohydrates – 4 g

Fat – 5 g

Protein – 24 g

Calories – 171

Ingredients:

- 1 pound firm white fish
- 3 tbsp soy sauce
- 2 tbsp rice wine
- 1 tbsp black bean paste
- 1 tsp minced ginger
- 1 tsp garlic
- 1 tbsp peanut oil
- a pinch of sliced green onions

Instructions:

1. Combine sauce ingredients and marinate the fish for 20-30 minutes.
2. Pour 2 cups of water into the pot.
3. Put the steamer inside.
4. Put fish in the basket.
5. Save the marinade.
6. Set to 2 minutes of low pressure.
7. Let the pressure release straight away.
8. Take out the fish and cover it with foil to keep warm.
9. Set to Saute and heat the oil.
10. Saute ginger for a few seconds.
11. Add the scallions and stir.
12. Pour in the saved marinade.
13. Boil the sauce until cooked.
14. Cover fish with sauce and top with green onion.
15. Enjoy!

Italian Tilapia

Prep time: 5 minutes

Cooking time: 4 minutes

Servings: 4

Nutrients per serving:

Carbohydrates – 2 g

Fat – 12 g

Protein – 20 g

Calories – 170

Ingredients:

- 4 tilapia fillets
- 3 tomatoes, diced
- 2 minced garlic cloves
- ¼ cup chopped basil
- 2 tbsp olive oil
- ½ cup of water
- ¼ tsp salt
- ⅛ tsp pepper

Instructions:

1. Add water to the pot.
2. Place the steamer basket into the pot.
3. Season the fish with salt and pepper and put into the basket.
4. Lock the lid and set the valve to Sealing.
5. Set to 4 minutes of high pressure (manual).
6. In a bowl, combine olive oil, tomatoes garlic. Set aside.
7. Do a quick-release when it's done.
8. Serve with the tomato mixture.
9. Enjoy!

Easy Fish

Prep time: 10 minutes

Cooking time: 15 minutes

Servings: 10

Nutrients per serving:

Carbohydrates – 12 g

Fat – 28 g

Protein – 2 g

Calories – 307

Ingredients:

- 12 cod fillets
- 2 tbsp lemon juice
- 6 tbsp butter
- 2 tsp oregano
- 28 ounces canned diced tomatoes
- Salt and pepper, to taste

Instructions:

1. Set to Saute and melt the butter.
2. Add all the ingredients except fish and cook for 10 minutes.
3. Put fish into the pot and cover with sauce.
4. Lock the lid.
5. Set to 5 minutes of high pressure (manual).
6. Let it release the pressure for 15 minutes.
7. Open the lid and take out the fish.
8. Enjoy!

Tilapia with Broccoli and Carrot

Prep time: 10 minutes

Cooking time: 10 minutes

Servings: 4

Nutrients per serving:

Carbohydrates – 50 g

Fat – 11 g

Protein – 29 g

Calories – 406

Ingredients:

- 1 pound tilapia fillets
- 2 carrots, cut into circles
- 3 cups broccoli florets
- 1 yellow squash, cut int circles
- ¼ tsp paprika
- ¼ tsp pepper
- 1 tsp salt
- ¼ cup of water
- a little piece of butter

Instructions:

1. Place sliced vegetables into the pot.
2. Put a trivet on top of vegetables.
3. Put fish on the trivet.
4. Cover the fish with water.
5. Combine spices and sprinkle each piece of fish.
6. Put a piece of butter on top of fillets.
7. Lock the lid and set the valve to Steam.
8. Set to 8 minutes of high pressure.
9. Quick-release the pressure when it's done.
10. Enjoy!

Indian Style Tilapia

Prep time: 5 minutes

Cooking time: 15 minutes

Servings: 4

Nutrients per serving:

Carbohydrates – 2 g

Fat – 4 g

Protein – 23 g

Calories – 160

Ingredients:

- 1½ pounds Fresh Tilapia Fillets
- 2 onion, chopped
- ⅓ cup tomato puree
- ½ tbsp ginger garlic
- ¼ tsp turmeric powder
- ½ tsp paprika powder
- ½ tsp cumin powder
- ½ tsp coriander powder
- 1 cup water
- 3 tbsp oil
- salt to taste
- a pinch of chopped parsley
- slice of lime

Instructions:

1. Set to Saute and heat the oil.
2. Add the onion and saute for a few minutes.
3. Add the ginger and garlic paste.
4. Add all the spices and tomato puree and cook for 2 minutes.
5. Add water.
6. Press Cancel.
7. Lock the lid and seal the valve.
8. Set 2 minutes of high pressure.
9. Do a quick release when it's done.
10. Add the fish into the pot.
11. Lock the lid and seal the valve.
12. Set to 1 minute high pressure.
13. Let the pressure naturally release.
14. Serve with parsley and a slice of lime.
15. Enjoy!

Lemon Fish

Prep time: 10 minutes

Cooking time: 10 minutes

Servings: 2

Nutrients per serving:

Carbohydrates – 0 g

Fat – 2 g

Protein – 23 g

Calories – 110

Ingredients:

- 2 tilapia or cod fillets
- 2 sprigs fresh dill
- 4 slices lemon
- 1 tbsp butter
- ½ tsp garlic powder
- salt to taste
- pepper to taste

Instructions:

1. Lay out 2 large squares of foil.
2. Put a fillet in the center of each foil square.
3. Season each piece of fish with salt, pepper, garlic powder.
4. Top fillets with 1 sprig of dill, 2 slices of lemon, and 1 tbsp of butter.
5. Place a trivet into the pressure cooker.
6. Add a cup of water to the pot.
7. Close up parchment paper around the fillets, folding to seal, and then place both packets on metal rack inside cooker.
8. Lock the lid and set to 5 minutes of high pressure.
9. Quick-release the pressure.
10. Serve as you like.
11. Enjoy!

Fishy Tortillas

Prep time: 10 minutes

Cooking time: 15 minutes

Servings: 2

Nutrients per serving:

Carbohydrates – 0 g

Fat – 2 g

Protein – 22 g

Calories – 110

Ingredients:

- 2 tilapia fillets
- 1 red pepper, chopped
- 1 tsp oil
- 2 tbsp smoked paprika
- Juice of 1 lime
- 2 tortillas
- 1½ cups of water
- Salt to taste

Instructions:

1. Put tilapia on a piece of parchment paper.
2. Season the fish with spices, oil and lime juice.
3. Fold the paper into a packet.
4. Add 1½ cups of water and trivet to the pot.
5. Put the packet on the trivet and lock the lid.
6. Cook at high pressure for 8 minutes.
7. Do a quick-release when it's done.
8. Fill tortillas with fish, pepper, your preferable sauce.
9. Enjoy!

Seasoned Cod Fillets

Prep time: 5 minutes

Cooking time: 10 minutes

Servings: 4

Nutrients per serving:

Carbohydrates –0 g

Fat – 1 g

Protein – 22 g

Calories – 85

Ingredients:

- 4 4-ounces cod fillet
- ½ cup hot water
- 6 tbsp butter
- 2 tsp minced garlic
- ½ tsp onion powder
- 1 tsp dried basil
- 1 tsp dried oregano
- Salt and pepper to taste
- Fresh parsley for serving

Instructions:

1. Set to Saute and melt the butter.
2. Add the minced garlic, onion powder, basil, and oregano and saute for a few minutes.
3. Remove mixture from pot and press Cancel.
4. Pour the hot water into the pot and put in the steamer rack.
5. Put the fillets on the steam rack and season them with salt and pepper.
6. Cover fillets with garlic mix.
7. Lock the lid and seal the valve.
8. Set to 2 minutes of Steam.
9. Quick-release the pressure.
10. Serve with fresh parsley.
11. Enjoy!

Cod with Cherry Tomatoes

Prep time: 10 minutes

Cooking time: 20 minutes

Servings: 3

Nutrients per serving:

Carbohydrates – 0 g

Fat – 1 g

Protein – 23 g

Calories – 95

Ingredients:

- 3 pieces frozen cod
- ½ tbsp butter
- ½ lemon juice
- ½ onion
- ½ tsp oregano
- 1 pound cherry tomatoes
- ½ tsp salt
- ¼ tsp black pepper
- a pinch of chopped parsley

Instructions:

1. Set to Saute and melt the butter.
2. Add all ingredients except fish to the pot and saute for 8-10 minutes.
3. Add fish to the pot and cover each piece with the sauce.
4. Lock the lid and seal the valve.
5. Set to 5 minutes of high pressure (manual).
6. Do a quick-release.
7. Enjoy!

SIDES AND PASTA

Perfect Rice

Prep time: 5 minutes

Cooking time: 22 minutes

Servings: 4

Nutrients per serving:

Carbohydrates – 36 g

Fat – 1 g

Protein – 3 g

Calories – 176

Ingredients:

- ½ tsp oil
- 1 cup brown rice or white rice
- 1 cup water
- ¼ tsp salt

Instructions:

1. Grease the pot with oil.
2. Rinse the rice under cold water, about 7 times.
3. Let it drain well and put in the pot.
4. Add water.
5. Lock the lid and set the valve to Sealing.
6. Set to 3 minutes for white rice or 22 for brown rice (pressure cook).
7. When finished cooking, let it release (10 minutes).
8. Do a quick release.
9. Enjoy!

Black Beans

Prep time: 10 minutes

Cooking time: 8 minutes

Servings: 2

Nutrients per serving:

Carbohydrates – 13 g

Fat – 2 g

Protein – 6 g

Calories – 67

Ingredients:

- 1 cup dried black beans
- ½ tsp salt
- 6 cups of water

Instructions:

1. Prepare the beans: rinse, drain, and pick over to remove debris.
2. Place the beans, salt, and water in the inner pot.
3. Lock the lid and set the valve to Sealing.
4. Set to 25 minutes of high pressure (manual).
5. Press Cancel and let it release, 30 minutes.
6. Unlock the lid.
7. If the beans aren't soft, set to Sauté (medium).
8. Let it boil and taste a bean every 5 minutes until it's soft enough.
9. Turn off the pot and wait until it cools.
10. Enjoy!

Red Potatoes

Prep time: 5 minutes

Cooking time: 12 minutes

Servings: 2

Nutrients per serving:

Carbohydrates – 20 g

Fat – 1 g

Protein – 3 g

Calories – 90

Ingredients:

- 1½ pounds medium red potatoes
- ¼ cup water
- ¼ cup butter
- 3 tbsp minced fresh parsley
- 1 tbsp lemon juice
- 1 tbsp minced chives
- Salt and pepper to taste

Instructions:

1. Add water and potatoes into the pot.
2. Lock lid and set to 12 minutes.
3. Do a quick-release when it's done.
4. Take out the potatoes and pour out the water.
5. Add potatoes and remaining ingredients to the pot, stir it well.
6. Enjoy!

Mashed Potatoes

Prep time: 10 minutes

Cooking time: 10 minutes

Servings: 6

Nutrients per serving:

Carbohydrates – 27 g

Fat – 4 g

Protein – 5 g

Calories – 142

Ingredients:

- 2 pounds Russet potatoes
- 3 cups water
- ⅓ cup milk
- ¼ cup light sour cream
- 2 tbsp butter
- ½ tsp salt
- Black pepper to taste
- a pinch of parsley

Instructions:

1. Put potatoes in the pot and cover with water.
2. Add salt.
3. Lock the and set to 10 minutes high pressure.
4. Do a quick-release when it's done.
5. Drain the water.
6. Add the butter, sour cream, milk, salt, black pepper.
7. Mash potatoes until smooth.
8. Enjoy!

Steamed Asparagus

Prep time: 5 minutes

Cooking time: 10 minutes

Servings: 4

Nutrients per serving:

Carbohydrates – 4 g

Fat – 1 g

Protein – 2 g

Calories – 23

Ingredients:

- 1 pound asparagus
- 1 cup of water
- Salt and black pepper to taste

Instructions:

1. Pour water into the pot and put the steamer rack inside.
2. Put the asparagus on the steamer rack.
3. Close the lid and set to 1 minute of high pressure.
4. Quick-release.
5. Season with salt and pepper.
6. Enjoy!

Pasta with Cheese and Chicken

Prep time: 10 minutes

Cooking time: 10 minutes

Servings: 5

Nutrients per serving:

Carbohydrates – 55 g

Fat – 13 g

Protein – 39 g

Calories – 500

Ingredients:

- 2 boneless, skinless chicken breasts
- 1 medium onion, chopped
- 2½-cans rotel
- ½ cup chicken broth
- 1 can (120 ml) cream of chicken soup
- ½ pound spaghetti
- ½ pound cheddar grated cheese
- a pinch of parsley

Instructions:

1. Put chicken, onion, and 1 cup of rotel in the pot.
2. Put spaghetti on top of everything.
3. Pour over the pasta with the rest rotel.
4. Combine cream of chicken soup and broth, then pour over spaghetti.
5. Close your lid and valve.
6. Set to 8 minutes of high pressure.
7. Do a quick release.
8. Set to Saute and add grated cheese to the pasta.
9. Stir until the sauce gets ticker.
10. Enjoy!

Penne Pasta and Sausage

Prep time: 10 minutes

Cooking time: 20 minutes

Servings: 6

Nutrients per serving:

Carbohydrates – 30 g

Fat – 7 g

Protein – 15 g

Calories – 229

Ingredients:

- 1 pound package sausage
- 1 onion, chopped
- 1 clove garlic, minced
- 1 tsp oil
- 3 cups chicken broth
- 12 ounces penne pasta
- 1 can diced tomatoes
- 2 tsp dried oregano
- 1 cup shredded cheddar cheese
- a pinch of chopped parsley

Instructions:

1. Set to Saute and heat the oil.
2. Saute the sausage and onion for a few minutes. Then add garlic.
3. Add chicken broth, pasta, tomatoes, and spices. Stir well.
4. Set to 5 minutes (manual).
5. Do a quick-release when it's done.
6. Set to Keep Warm and add the cheese.
7. Left for 10-15 minutes.
8. Serve with chopped parsley.
9. Enjoy!

Pasta with Pesto Sauce

Prep time: 5 minutes

Cooking time: 15 minutes

Servings: 3

Nutrients per serving:

Carbohydrates – 68 g

Fat – 29 g

Protein – 14 g

Calories – 594

Ingredients:

- 1 tbsp oil
- ½ pound spaghetti
- 2 cup water
- ¾ cup pesto
- Basil leaves for serving

Instructions:

1. Put spaghetti inside the pot and cover with water.
2. Add the oil.
3. Lock the lid and set the vent to Sealing.
4. Set to 4 minutes of high pressure (manual).
5. Do a quick release.
6. Add pesto to pasta and stir.
7. Serve with basil leaves.
8. Enjoy!

Spring Vegetable Pasta

Prep time: 10 minutes

Cooking time: 5 minutes

Servings: 4

Nutrients per serving:

Carbohydrates – 40 g

Fat – 8 g

Protein – 11 g

Calories – 268

Ingredients:

- 12 ounces penne pasta
- 2 cups water or chicken broth
- 1 pint cherry tomatoes
- 12 ounces frozen vegetables
- 2 tbsp butter
- 2 cloves garlic, minced
- ½ tsp salt
- Fresh basil leaves

Instructions:

1. Set to Saute and melt the butter.
2. Press Cancel.
3. Add pasta, water or broth, and salt.
4. Add minced garlic, tomatoes, basil, and vegetables.
5. Lock the lid and set to 2 minutes of high pressure.
6. When it's done, do a quick-release.
7. Enjoy!

Creamy Garlic Pasta

Prep time: 15 minutes

Cooking time: 20 minutes

Servings: 4

Nutrients per serving:

Carbohydrates – 35 g

Fat – 40 g

Protein – 23 g

Calories – 596

Ingredients:

- 2 large boneless, skinless chicken breasts
- 8 ounces dried fettuccine pasta
- 2 tbsp olive oil
- ½ cups water
- 1 jar (1 pound) Alfredo sauce
- 1 cup of shredded mozzarella or parmesan cheese
- 4 cloves garlic, minced
- ½ tsp salt
- a handful of chopped parsley

Instructions:

1. Set to Sauté and heat the oil.
2. Brown chicken.
3. Add the garlic.
4. Season with salt and stir well.
5. When the meat is cooked, press Cancel.
6. Add ½ cup of water and the Alfredo sauce and mix well.
7. Put the fettuccine over the chicken mixture.
8. Cover the pasta with water.
9. Lock the lid.
10. Set to 8 minutes of high pressure (manual) pressure.
11. When it's done, quick release the pressure.
12. Add cheese to pasta and lock the lid.
13. Let the sauce thicken.
14. Serve with chopped parsley.
15. Enjoy!

ASIAN MEALS

Sesamed Beef and Broccoli

Prep time: 10 minutes

Cooking time: 12 minutes

Servings: 4

Nutrients per serving:

Carbohydrates – 17 g

Fat – 18 g

Protein – 31 g

Calories – 354

Ingredients:

- 1¼ pounds boneless beef chuck roast
- ⅛ tsp salt
- ¼ tsp black pepper
- ½ tsp sesame oil
- 2 cloves garlic minced
- ½ tsp grated ginger
- 3½ cups broccoli florets
- ⅓ cup soy sauce
- ⅔ cup beef broth
- 2 tbsp oyster sauce
- 3 tbsp brown sugar
- 1½ tsp sesame oil
- 2½ tbsp cornstarch
- 3 tbsp water
- a pinch of sesame seeds

Instructions:

1. Set to Saute and heat the oil.
2. Brown all sides of the seasoned beef with salt and pepper.

3. Add garlic and ginger.
4. In a small bowl, combine the broth, soy and oyster sauce, brown sugar, sesame oil.
5. Add broccoli and cover the meat with the mixture.
6. Turn off the Saute.
7. Lock the lid and set the valve to Sealing.
8. Set to 6 minutes of high pressure (manual).
9. Quick-release when the beef is cooked.
10. Combine the cornstarch and water and pour in the pot.
11. Set to Saute and let the sauce thicken.
12. Sprinkle with sesame seeds.
13. Enjoy!

Five-Minutes Noodle

Prep time: 10 minutes

Cooking time: 5 minutes

Servings: 4

Nutrients per serving:

Carbohydrates – 54 g

Fat – 5 g

Protein – 11 g

Calories – 299

Ingredients:

- ½ pound pasta
- 1 cup peas
- 1 cup broccoli florets
- 2 carrots, sliced
- 1½ cups chicken broth
- 1 garlic clove
- 1 tbsp sesame oil
- 1 tsp grated ginger
- 2 tbsp soy sauce
- 1 tbsp oyster sauce
- 1 tbsp brown sugar

Instructions:

1. Set to Saute and heat the sesame oil.
2. Add garlic and saute for a few minutes.
3. Put the noodles on the bottom of the pot and put the vegetables on top.
4. Combine chicken broth, ginger, soy sauce, oyster sauce, rice wine, brown sugar. Pour in the mixture into the pot.
5. Seal and set to 5 minutes of high pressure (manual).
6. Do a quick-release when finished.
7. Unlock the lid and stir.
8. Enjoy!

Homemade Ramen

Prep time: 10 minutes

Cooking time: 15 minutes

Servings: 6

Nutrients per serving:

Carbohydrates – 31 g

Fat – 16 g

Protein – 29 g

Calories – 369

Ingredients:

- 1 pound chicken tenders or chicken breasts
- 1½ tbsp oil
- 4 cups chicken broth
- 2 cups water
- 4 medium eggs
- 3 packages ramen noodles
- 2 tbsp soy sauce
- a handful of chopped green onion
- Salt to taste
- Black pepper to taste
- Few drops chili oil

Instructions:

1. Sprinkle the chicken with salt and black pepper.
2. Set to Saute and heat the oil.
3. Brown chicken.
4. Add the chicken broth and water.
5. Lock the lid and set to 10 minutes of high pressure (manual).
6. Do a quick release and take out the chicken.
7. Shred the meat with forks.
8. Set to Saute mode and bring to a boil.
9. Add chicken and ramen noodles.
10. Add green onion and soy sauce when the ramen is soft. Stir.
11. Serve with ramen eggs, and chili oil.
12. Enjoy!

Asian Style Fish

Prep time: 5 minutes

Cooking time: 15 minutes

Servings: 4

Nutrients per serving:

Carbohydrates – 30 g

Fat – 9 g

Protein – 32 g

Calories – 430

Ingredients:

- 2 white fish fillets
- 1 cup vegetable or chicken broth
- 1-inch piece of fresh ginger
- 1 clove garlic
- 1 tsp soy sauce
- 1 tbsp butter
- 1½ tsp miso paste
- ¼ lemon
- 1 medium bunch kale
- Salt and pepper to taste

Instructions:

1. Add broth, ginger, and garlic to the pot.
2. Put the trivet inside the pot and cover it with foil.
3. Put the fish on the foil and top with soy sauce.
4. Lock the lid.
5. Set to 10 minutes of low pressure.
6. Combine the butter and miso and set aside.
7. Do a quick-release when it's done.
8. Drizzle lemon juice over the fillets.
9. Take out the trivet and set to Saute.
10. Add the kale and cook for a 2-3 minutes.
11. Press Cancel.
12. Sprinkle the fillets with salt and pepper.
13. Put the fillets on the kale and cover with miso-butter sauce.
14. Enjoy!

Teriyaki Pork

Prep time: 10 minutes

Cooking time: 35 minutes

Servings: 10

Nutrients per 4 ounces cooked pork:

Carbohydrates – 7 g

Fat – 6 g

Protein – 27 g

Calories – 198

Ingredients:

- 1 boneless pork loin roast
- ¾ cup apple juice
- 2 tbsp sugar
- 2 tbsp teriyaki sauce
- 2 tbsp soy sauce
- 1 tbsp white vinegar
- 1 tsp ground ginger
- ¼ tsp garlic powder
- ⅛ tsp pepper
- 8 tsp cornstarch
- 3 tbsp water

Instructions:

1. Add apple juice, sugar, teriyaki, soy sauce, vinegar, and spices to the pot.
2. Put the roast into the mixture.
3. Lock the lid and the valve.
4. Set to 30 minutes high pressure (manual).
5. When it's done, do a quick-release (10 minutes)
6. Take out the meat.
7. Combine cornstarch with water and stir.
8. Add it to the pot.
9. Set to Saute (low).
10. Let the sauce thicken.
11. Serve pork with sauce.
12. Enjoy!

Stewed Asian Pork

Prep time: 25 minutes

Cooking time: 1-¼ hours + releasing minutes

Servings: 8

Nutrients per serving:

Carbohydrates – 27 g

Fat – 18 g

Protein – 31 g

Calories – 392

Ingredients:

- ½ cup honey
- ½ cup hoisin sauce
- ¼ cup soy sauce
- ¼ cup teriyaki sauce
- ¼ cup ketchup
- 4 garlic cloves
- 4 tsp fresh ginger, minced
- 1 tsp Chinese five-spice powder
- 1 boneless pork shoulder roast
- ½ cup chicken broth
- a pinch of sesame seeds
- a handful of chopped green onion

Instructions:

1. Mix honey, hoisin, soy sauce, ketchup, garlic, ginger, and spices in a zip-lock bag.
2. Cut roast in half and put in bag, coating in marinade. Refrigerate overnight.
3. Transfer pork and marinade to the pot.
4. Add chicken broth.
5. Lock the lid and the valve.
6. Set to 1 hour 15 minutes high pressure (manual).
7. Let it release the pressure (10 minutes).
8. Do a quick-release next.
9. Take out the meat and shred it.
10. Sprinkle with sesame seeds and green onion.
11. Enjoy!

Chicken with Teriyaki Sauce

Prep time: 5 minutes

Cooking time: 6 minutes

Servings: 4

Nutrients per serving:

Carbohydrates – 17 g

Fat – 12 g

Protein – 34 g

Calories – 298

Ingredients:

- 1½ pound boneless, skinless chicken thighs
- 1½ tbsp cooking oil
- 2½ tbsp soy sauce
- ½ cup mirin
- 1½ tbsp sugar
- 1 tbsp water
- 1 tsp corn starch
- a pinch of sesame seeds

Instructions:

1. Set to Saute and heat the oil.
2. Brown the chicken lightly.
3. Add the soy sauce, mirin, and sugar.
4. Lock the lid and set to 6 minutes high pressure (manual).
5. Do a quick-release when it's done.
6. Set to Saute.
7. Stir together cornstarch and water, then add to pot.
8. Let the sauce thicken.
9. Sprinkle the chicken with sesame seeds.
10. Enjoy!

Asian Rice

Prep time: 5 minutes

Cooking time: 28 minutes

Servings: 4

Nutrients per serving:

Carbohydrates – 40 g

Fat – 2 g

Protein – 3 g

Calories – 187

Ingredients:

- 1 cup white basmati rice
- 1 cup vegetable broth or stock
- ½ tsp Chinese five-spice powder
- 2 tsp sesame oil
- 2 tsp soy sauce
- a pinch of chopped parsley or spring onions
- 1 chilis

Instructions:

1. Put all ingredients, except spring onions and chilis, into the pressure pot.
2. Lock the lid and the vent.
3. Set to 3 minutes high pressure + keep warm.
4. Let it release for 25 minutes.
5. Do a quick release next.
6. Serve with chopped green onion and chiles.
7. Enjoy!

Box Soy Noodles

Prep time: 5 minutes

Cooking time: 15 minutes

Servings: 4

Nutrients per serving:

Carbohydrates – 30 g

Fat – 9 g

Protein – 32 g

Calories – 430

Ingredients:

- ½ cup soy sauce
- 2 tbsp rice vinegar
- 2 tbsp butter
- 2 tbsp erythritol
- 2 cups chicken broth
- 1 pound boneless skinless chicken breast, chopped
- 2 large carrots, chopped
- 1 pepper, chopped
- ½ pound uncooked wheat noodles
- a handful of chopped parsley

Instructions:

1. Put chicken, noodles, vegetables and the rest of ingredients in the pot.
2. Lock the lid and the vent.
3. Set to 3 minutes of high pressure (manual).
4. When finished, do a quick release.
5. Serve with chopped parsley.
6. Enjoy!

Asian Chicken Wings

Prep time: 10 minutes

Cooking time: 10 minutes

Servings: 3

Nutrients per serving:

Carbohydrates – 19 g

Fat – 26 g

Protein – 24 g

Calories – 409

Ingredients:

- 1½ pounds chicken wings
- 1 tbsp oil
- 1-inch piece ginger
- 2 tbsp soy light sauce
- 3 tbsp soy dark sauce
- 3 dashes ground white pepper
- ½ cup water
- 1 tsp sesame oil
- a handful of chopped green onion

Instructions:

1. Set to Saute and add the oil.
2. Brown the chicken wings.
3. Add the ginger and saute for a few minutes.
4. Add the soy sauce, sesame oil, pepper, and water.
5. Lock the lid and set to 8 minutes of high pressure (manual).
6. Do a quick-release.
7. Stir and serve with chopped green onion.
8. Enjoy!

DESSERTS

Cheesecake

Prep time: 20 minutes

Cooking time: 60 minutes + cooling

Servings: 3

Nutrients per serving:

Carbohydrates – 39 g

Fat – 34 g

Protein – 8 g

Calories – 484

Ingredients:

- 1 cup water
- ¾ cup graham cracker crumbs
- 1 tbsp plus ⅔ cup sugar
- ¼ tsp ground cinnamon
- 2½ tbsp butter, melted
- 16 ounces cream cheese
- 2 tsp vanilla extract
- 2 eggs

Instructions:

1. Grease a cake pan.
2. Add water to the pot.
3. In a bowl, combine melted butter the cracker crumbs, 1 tbsp sugar, cinnamon.
4. Press onto bottom of prepared pan.
5. Whisk the cream cheese and remaining sugar until smooth.
6. Slowly whisk in vanilla and eggs.
7. Pour over crust.
8. Cover the pan with foil.
9. Put cake pan on the trivet with handles and place inside the pot.
10. Lock the lid and closed the vent.
11. Set to 1 hour and 5 minutes low pressure (manual).
12. Do a quick-release when it's done.
13. The cheesecake should be jiggly but set in the center.
14. Let the cheesecake cool for 1 hour.
15. Place it in the fridge to chill overnight.
16. Enjoy!

Chocolate Cake with Raspberries

Prep time: 10 minutes

Cooking time: 25 minutes

Servings: 6

Nutrients per serving:

Carbohydrates – 58 g

Fat – 22 g

Protein – 3 g

Calories – 424

Ingredients:

- 1 cup water
- 4 large eggs
- 1½ cups sugar
- ½ cup butter
- 1 tbsp vanilla extract
- 1 cup flour
- ½ cup baking cocoa
- 1 tbsp instant coffee granules
- a handful of raspberries
- ¼ tsp salt

Instructions:

1. Add water to the pot.
2. Blend together eggs, sugar, butter, and vanilla in one bowl.
3. Mix the flour, cocoa, coffee granules, and salt in another bowl. Then slowly add to egg mixture.
4. Put mixture in a greased 1½ -qt. baking dish and cover with foil.
5. Put the dish on the trivet and place it inside the pot.
6. Lock the lid and the vent.
7. Set to 25 minutes of high pressure (manual).
8. Let it release for 10 minutes.
9. Do a quick-release.
10. Check the cake with a toothpick.
11. Serve with raspberries.
12. Enjoy!

Crusty Cherry Pie

Prep time: 10 minutes

Cooking time: 40 minutes

Servings: 2

Nutrients per serving:

Carbohydrates – 8 g

Fat – 24 g

Protein – 8 g

Calories – 180

Ingredients:

- 20 ounce cherry pie filling
- ¾ cup sugar
- ¾ cup flour
- 6 tbsp butter
- 1 tsp vanilla extract
- 1 cup of water
- ¼ tsp salt

Instructions:

1. Add water to the pot.
2. Put down the trivet.
3. Grease a cake pan.
4. Pour the filling into the cake pan.
5. Combine the sugar, flour, and salt in a bowl.
6. Melt the butter.
7. Gradually add the butter and vanilla extract to the dry ingredients.

8. Mix until dough forms.
9. Squeeze teaspoons of dough into a ball. Then flatten into a round.
10. Place on top of the filling.
11. Place a paper towel on top of the cake pan and cover tightly with foil.
12. Place the pan inside the pot carefully.
13. Lock the lid and set the vent to Sealing.
14. Set to 30 minutes of high pressure.
15. Do a quick-release.
16. Let it cool.
17. Enjoy!

Chocolate Brownie

Prep time: 5 minutes

Cooking time: 20 minutes

Servings: 10

Nutrients per serving:

Carbohydrates – 32 g

Fat – 12 g

Protein – 2 g

Calories – 242

Ingredients:

- ⅓ cup oil
- ⅓ cup pumpkin puree
- ⅓ cup milk
- 2 tbsp apple sauce
- 1 tsp vanilla extract
- ½ cup sugar
- ¾ cup all-purpose flour
- 3 tbsp cocoa powder
- 1 tsp baking powder
- 1 tsp pumpkin pie spice
- pinch of salt
- 1½ cups water
- butter to grease the cake tin

Instructions:

1. Grease the cake tin with butter.
2. Combine the oil, pumpkin puree, apple sauce, vanilla extract, milk, and sugar in a bowl.
3. Add the remaining ingredients and mix until just combined.
4. Add the mixture to the tin and cover with foil.
5. Place the tin on the trivet.
6. Add water to the pot.
7. Put the trivet with the covered brownie cake tin to the pot.
8. Lock the lid and set the vent to Sealing.
9. Set to 20 minutes of high pressure (manual).
10. Let it release the pressure for 20 minutes.
11. Enjoy!

Strawberry Biscuit

Prep time: 5 minutes

Cooking time: 5 minutes

Servings: 2

Nutrients per serving:

Carbohydrates – 84 g

Fat – 13 g

Protein – 6 g

Calories – 468

Ingredients:

- 1¼ cups flour
- ½ cup sugar
- 2 tsp baking powder
- ¾ cups milk
- ⅓ cup butter
- 1 tsp vanilla extract
- 1 cup strawberries, chopped
- butter to grease baking dish

Instructions:

1. Blend the flour, sugar, and baking powder.
2. Slowly add the milk, melted butter, and vanilla extract.
3. Add the strawberries.
4. Grease baking dish with butter and transfer the butter into it.
5. Put the trivet into the pot.
6. Pour in 1 cup of water.
7. Place the baking dish on the trivet and secure the lid.
8. Set to 12 minutes of high pressure.
9. Let it release for 10-15 minutes.
10. Enjoy!

Crustless Mini Cheesecake

Prep time: 10 minutes

Cooking time: 1 hour + cooling

Servings: 4

Nutrients per serving:

Carbohydrates – 3 g

Fat – 3 g

Protein – 6 g

Calories – 59

Ingredients:

- 14 ounce condensed milk
- 1 cup whole milk yogurt
- Butter to grease egg mold

Instructions:

1. Combine the condensed milk and yogurt.
2. Put the mixture into a egg mold and cover with foil.
3. Add 2 cups water to the pot and put the trivet down.
4. Place the egg mold on top of the rack.
5. Lock the lid and the valve.
6. Set to 30 minutes at high pressure.
7. Let it release the pressure (20 minutes).
8. Do a quick release next.
9. Let the cakes cool down.
10. Put them in the fridge to chill for 6 hours.
11. Enjoy!

CONCLUSION

Thank you for reading this book and having the patience to try the recipes.

I do hope that you have had as much enjoyment reading and experimenting with the meals as I have had writing the book.

If you would like to leave a comment, you can do so at the Order section->Digital orders, in your Amazon account.

Stay safe and healthy!

Recipe Index

Conversion Tables

VOLUME EQUIVALENTS (LIQUID)

US STANDARD	US STANDARD (OUNCES)	METRIC
2 tablespoons	1 fl. oz.	30 mL
¼ cup	2 fl. oz.	60 mL
½ cup	4 fl. oz.	120 mL
1 cup	8 fl. oz.	240mL
1½ cups	12 fl. oz.	355 mL
2 cups or 1 pint	16 fl. oz.	475 mL
4 cups or 1 quart	32 fl. oz.	1 L
1 gallon	128 fl. oz.	4 L

OVEN TEMPERATURES

FAHRENHEIT (°F)	CELSIUS (°C) APPROXIMATE
250 °F	120 °C
300 °F	150 °C
325 °F	165 °C
350 °F	180 °C
375 °F	190 °C
400 °F	200 °C
425 °F	220 °C
450 °F	230 °C

VOLUME EQUIVALENTS (LIQUID)

US STANDARD	METRIC (APPROXIMATE)
⅛ teaspoon	0.5 mL
¼ teaspoon	1 mL
½ teaspoon	2 mL
⅔ teaspoon	4 mL
1 teaspoon	5 mL
1 tablespoon	15 mL
¼ cup	59 mL
⅓ cup	79 mL
½ cup	118 mL
⅔ cup	156 mL
¾ cup	177 mL
1 cup	235 mL
2 cups or 1 pint	475 mL
3 cups	700 mL
4 cups or 1 quart	1 L
½ gallon	2 L
1 gallon	4 L

WEIGHT EQUIVALENTS

US STANDARD	METRIC (APPROXIMATE)
½ ounce	15 g
1 ounce	30 g
2 ounces	60 g
4 ounces	115 g
8 ounces	225 g
12 ounces	340 g
16 ounces or 1 pound	455 g

Other Books by Tiffany Shelton

Tiffany Shelton's page on Amazon

Made in the USA
Middletown, DE
21 December 2020

29656498R00051